Unseen Victories

Finding Joy in the Journey

By

Juliet Agocha

Dedication

It can be tough to keep going when nobody acknowledges your victories, no matter how small they may seem. But remember, your accomplishments are not defined by the recognition they receive. They are valid and important, even if nobody else sees them.

To anyone who is striving for greatness and pushing forward, even if nobody applauds you, this book is dedicated to you.

Contents

Acknowledgements

The world is better because people want to grow and lead others. What makes it even better is that people give the gift of their time to teach future leaders. Thank you to everyone who seeks to improve themselves and others. It is the definition of the book "Unseen Victories."

I want to thank EVERYONE who has inspired me, encouraged me, or said something positive. This book would not be possible without the experiences and support of my team at Ultimate Web Design. You have given me the opportunity to lead a fantastic group of people-being a leader of outstanding leaders is a blessing.

Developing an idea into a phenomenal book is as difficult as it sounds. The experience is both mentally demanding and satisfying.

I thank the Sovereign LORD for the power, grace, and insight to write this book. My heartfelt gratitude goes to my husband, Zebulon Agocha; my daughters, Angel, and Heaven; my son, Ihichi; and my mother, Irene Ike.

Foreword

It has been my pleasure to have known Juliet Agocha since 2009, a friendship that went from mere acquaintance to partnership in academics and ministry.

I have seen her grow in her relationship with Jesus Christ to the point that her heart burns with the desire to go deeper and deeper in the knowledge of the beauty of the Lord.

I have seen her consistency and passion for helping men and women to overcome obstacles and life challenges. I am grateful for the positive impacts Juliet has made on the younger generation and the community- Min. Joy Steven

Preface

The struggle of going unnoticed for everyday successes delves into the often-unseen achievements that go underappreciated in our daily lives.

From small wins at work to personal milestones, this book explores the emotional toll of not receiving recognition for our efforts. Join me as we navigate the complex world of Unseen Victories and the importance of acknowledging our own successes, even when others may not.

Don't let your achievements go unrecognized any longer. Discover the power of "Unseen

Victories" to celebrate the wins that truly matter. Because at the end of the day, the only validation you truly need is from yourself.

Unseen Victories?

The Overlooked Wins That Shape Our Lives

WE ALL HAVE OUR share of victories and achievements in life, big and small. Yet often the smallest of wins go unnoticed or unappreciated, both by others and ourselves. These are what I call our "unseen victories" the everyday accomplishments, acts of progress and courage, moments of learning and growth that silently shape our days yet rarely get celebrated. Finishing a difficult work project, having a breakthrough in understanding something new, overcoming a long-held fear, helping someone in need, sticking to a health goal these unseen victories may not win medals or make headlines, but they impact our lives in powerful ways.

Diminishing Our Own Achievements

The problem is we tend to brush past these small wins, diminishing their significance in light of grander goals and dreams. We downplay the effort it took to achieve them, telling ourselves "it's no big deal." But it IS a big deal. Our self-growth and self-esteem often depend more on these incremental unseen victories than we realize. Tiny gains in knowledge and competence compound over time to build confidence and skill. Small acts of courage chip away at self-doubt. Each time we prevail over procrastination, stay true to our values, or lend a helping hand, it makes us a little stronger and wiser.

The Power of Appreciating Small Achievements

This book explores why we should pay more attention to life's unseen victories and learn to better celebrate our everyday accomplishments, no matter how minor they may seem. Appreciating our efforts, embracing our progress, and patting ourselves on the back along the way is key to motivation, happiness and self-fulfillment. By focusing on unseen victories, we can transform our mindset, boost positiviry in our daily lives, and uncover the incredible power of small achievements.

Inspiring Greater Self-Appreciation

My goal is to open your eyes to the wins hiding in plain sight around you and inspire you to honor your personal growth journey. For in those quiet, unrewarded moments of perseverance, courage, kindness and triumph, our best selves emerge one tiny victory at a time. When we take time to recognize and celebrate these unseen wins, we nurture greater confidence, resilience and wisdom to take on life's bigger challenges.

Boosting Happiness And Well-Being

LIFE'S SMALL WINS AND everyday accomplishments are easy to brush past without much thought. Yet taking time to recognize these unseen victories provides a wellspring of positive emotions that boost our spirits and fuel our drive. Appreciating our efforts and honoring our own growth fosters feelings of joy, gratitude, satisfaction and pride.

Noticing the Small Stuff

Joy surfaces when we take time to notice, appreciate and even celebrate life's smaller triumphs. Completing a workout, learning a new skill, sticking to a finance goal these small wins deserve recognition. By stopping to acknowledge our efforts, progress and daily achievements, we give ourselves permission to feel good about our actions.

Feeling Grateful for Growth

Seeing our small accomplishments also cultivates gratitude. When we observe our own effort and willingness to learn, overcome challenges and prevail over obstacles, it sparks thankfulness for our grit, courage and growth. Gratitude fills us when we honor the path we've traveled and use small victories to mark our positive expansion.

Satisfaction from Accomplishment

Even minor triumphs and tasks completed generate satisfaction. Checking off that nagging chore, having the discipline to exercise before work, figuring out a solution to a problem unseen victories such as these instill a sense of accomplishment. When we validate our efforts by acknowledging these micro-wins, we reap the emotional reward of satisfaction.

Pride in Ourselves

As everyday victories stack up, they gradually transform our self-perception bolstering confidence, resilience and pride in our abilities. The competencies we build through repetitively confronting challenges and having micro-successes shape our identity over time. By honoring our unsung daily wins, we nurture deepening pride in who we are becoming the heroes of our own small achievements.

How Unseen Victories Ease Stress and Anxiety

In addition to boosting positive feelings, taking time to acknowledge the small wins in life can also minimize negative emotions like stress, anxiety, frustration and guilt. Celebrating unseen victories provides a buffer against these troubling feelings.

Relieving Stress in the Moment

When tension builds from a difficult day and we feel swamped by pressures, taking a pause to appreciate an unseen victory can relieve stress. Whether it's completing a presentation, having a win with a child or taking time for self-care, highlighting little accomplishments creates breathing room for a stressed mind.

Building Resilience to Anxiety

Seeing daily achievements also fortifies resilience against future anxiety. Completing an unpleasant chore, having an uncomfortable conversation or facing a fear might unfold as unseen victories. Honoring these small acts of courage reminds us we can handle hard things, equipping us with greater calm and confidence moving ahead.

Releasing Frustrations Bit by Bit

In the face of exasperating tasks, honoring mini-wins helps dissipate frustrations before they fully form. Making any degree of progress breaking an assignment into steps, grasping a new skill, pushing past confusion to gain understanding is victory. Validating small gains releases air from the balloon of frustration.

Alleviating the Burden of Guilt

When self-criticism and perfectionism take hold, unseen victories also lift the weight of guilt. Finding compassion for our efforts, whether or not they meet idealized standards, brings self-forgiveness. We release perceived failures when we celebrate unseen wins buried in the debris of guilt. For life is complex, and victory lives in the small steps forward.

How Unseen Victories Nurture Inner Growth

Celebrating small, everyday accomplishments is a pathway to nurturing our core psychological needs including the needs for autonomy, competence and relatedness. Appreciating our efforts and honoring our determination fuels intrinsic growth in profound ways.

Nurturing Autonomy

Pursuing an unseen victory often requires exercising autonomy, acting from internal drive and values vs. external pressures. Completing a passion project, cultivating a new skill, making time for self-care over other demands these achievements reflect us acting as our authentic selves. Pausing to acknowledge these small wins affirms our self-directedness. We feel energized about owning our path when we celebrate the autonomy embedded in our quiet victories.

Strengthening Competence

Each small achievement and instance of progress learning new information, troubleshooting an issue, pushing beyond obstacles builds competence. Competence grows from reveling in effort and celebrating the skill-building that happens with each unseen victory. Reminding ourselves "I struggled, I learned, I now know how to do this" fosters self-efficacy. Honoring the competence within micro-wins drives motivation and joy.

Deepening Relatedness

Even victories cloaked in solitude can nurture relatedness and shared humanity. The awareness that others have likely experienced similar wins and losses builds feeling connected. We realize that every person faces unseen victories and unseen challenges daily. Investigating how our smaller triumphs tie us to the broader human experience combats loneliness. Regardless of external praise, we share in the journey of progress and setbacks across humanity.

Easing Grief and Disappointment

In the journey of life, we all face moments that test our resilience and shake the very foundations of our being. Among these challenges are the deep valleys of grief, the sharp pains of disappointment, and the heart-wrenching turmoil of broken relationships. While these experiences may seem insurmountable, there lies a subtle yet powerful force within us all that can help pave the path to healing: the recognition and celebration of unseen victories. These are the small, personal triumphs that often go unnoticed by the world but hold the power to transform our internal landscape.

Healing from Grief

The process of healing from grief is a deeply personal journey, one that unfolds in its own time and often in unexpected ways. For those who have lost loved ones to circumstances as heart-wrenching as cancer or suicide, the path forward may seem shrouded in darkness. Yet, within this darkness, there exist glimmers of light - unseen victories that gradually lead to healing.

One such victory might be found in the ability to remember and speak of the deceased with a smile, rather than through tears alone. It's a significant step, marking a transition from mourning their absence to celebrating their life and the memories shared. Another victory is in the re-engagement with the world, perhaps through returning to a hobby or activity that was once enjoyed together. It doesn't signify moving on but moving forward, carrying their memory into new experiences.

Community and support groups play a crucial role in this aspect of healing, offering a space to share stories and memories, thus normalizing the grief experience. Engaging with others who have walked similar paths can illuminate the small steps of progress that might otherwise go unnoticed. These interactions often act as milestones of healing, underscoring the importance of connection and shared understanding.

Healing from Disappointment

Disappointment, especially when it stems from deep personal aspirations or professional endeavors, can be a profound source of distress. However, the journey through disappointment is also ripe with opportunities for growth and self-reflection. Recognizing the value of reevaluation and adjustment stands as a silent victory in the aftermath of unmet expectations.

One unseen victory is the courage to reassess and redefine success on one's own terms. This might mean setting new, perhaps more realistic goals or finding value in the journey itself rather than the outcome. The act of resilience, of not letting disappointment deter one from continuing to strive, is a monumental achievement that often goes unrecognized.

Furthermore, the experience of disappointment often leads to enhanced emotional intelligence. The introspection it encourages can deepen one's understanding of their emotional landscape, improving how they handle future setbacks and navigate the complexities of their aspirations. This enhanced emotional resilience turns the pain of disappointment into a powerful catalyst for personal development.

Healing from Broken Relationships

The end of a significant relationship can feel like a profound loss, akin to grieving. Yet, within this loss, there is ample space for personal growth and the rediscovery of self. An unseen victory in this context is the gradual return to self-sufficiency, finding joy and contentment in one's own company, and rekindling interests and passions that may have been neglected.

Another significant step is the rebuilding of trust, not just in others but in oneself. This involves recognizing the strength that comes from surviving heartbreak and the wisdom gained from introspection about what one truly values in a relationship. Each small realization and act of self-care is a victory, marking progress on the journey to healing.

Embracing vulnerability again, perhaps through new friendships or interests, is a testament to the resilience of the human spirit. It signifies not a replacement of what was lost but an expansion of the heart's capacity to love and connect. This openness to new experiences and people can transform the way one views relationships, leading to deeper, more meaningful connections in the future.

The path through grief, disappointment, and broken relationships is fraught with challenges, but it is also lined with countless unseen victories. These milestones, though small, are significant markers of progress, resilience, and personal growth. By acknowledging and celebrating these victories, individuals can navigate their pain with grace and emerge with a renewed sense of self, ready to face the future with hope and openness.

The Power of Appreciating Progress

The notion that honoring small wins and incremental growth is pivotal for wellbeing and performance finds support in research: In a study of over 500 people pursuing goals, those who focused on "progress framing" appreciating small advances put in more effort and achieved greater success over months than those fixated on achievement framing. Tracking and celebrating progress fuels motivation.

The Compounding Effect of Small Wins

Scientists find that celebrating micro-wins and small acts of willpower strengthens self-control and determination over time, essential for achieving longer-term goals. Praising ourselves along the way builds grit. One study showed that participants who focused on their progress rather than results managed 50% higher rates of exercise over a 2-month period. Small fitness victories compound. Researchers looking at savings goals found that people noting incremental progress put away 82% more money over a 6-month timeframe than those ignoring interim milestones. Progress ignites momentum.

Micro-Wins Cultivate Wellbeing

Multiple studies link gratitude for personal growth experiences progress on goals, gaining knowledge, showing self-restraint to heightened life satisfaction and decreased depression. Honoring unseen victories elevates wellbeing. Scientists have discovered expressing pride in our efforts, regardless of the outcome, activates reward centers in the brain, flooding us with dopamine and driving further goal-pursuit. Celebrating progress feels good! Workers who took a moment to recognize their efforts and wins, however small, were found to have 23% lower stress hormone levels and feel more engaged, energized about their tasks and open to learning. The numbers confirm that by focusing more attention on the small, incremental wins hiding in plain sight around us, we magnify the positive strengthening inner reserves and supporting success on all scales. Our unseen victories constitute a vital force for realizing potential.

Conclusion

& we journey through life, seeking to grow, achieve, and contribute, it is human nature to fixate on the big wins the new job, the degree, the race medal. Yet in doing so, we overlook an incredible power source that charges our growth from the inside out the power of life's unseen victories. The small wins that shape our hours and days carry more potential than we realize. Each time we stick to a goal, show courage, prevail over self-doubt, help others, or celebrate progress, we build emotional resilience, self-efficacy, compassion and wisdom.

Research confirms that recognizing these micro-achievements amplifies motivation and wellbeing. By focusing more attention on the unsung accomplishments hiding in plain sight, we gain energy, direction and strength for the longer-term challenges.

Within every unseen victory no matter how minor we have the chance to honor grit, effort and self-expansion. We have the opportunity to feel dignity, pride, joy and gratitude for the learning and progress etched into each small win. We have the opening to recognize ourselves as the heroes authoring our growth stories, one quietly courageous step at a time. & this book details, there is incredible power within reach if we wake up to the victory narrative already unfolding each day through our

small achievements. For in celebrating the unseen wins along the way, we build lives truly
worth celebrating, from the inside out.

Confidence And Self-Worth Enhancer

FEW THINGS ARE MORE essential to happiness and fulfillment than believing in ourselves and feeling worthy. Self-confidence and healthy self-esteem allow us to act on goals, handle setbacks, and form meaningful connections with others. Yet many of us struggle at times with self-doubt, harsh inner critics, or feelings of inadequacy draining motivation and leading to withdrawal. The good news is that confidence and self-worth can be strengthened through life's many unseen victories.

In this chapter, we see how progress, effort and perseverance in the small domains of life build an inner foundation of confidence and value. Each time we overcome inertia to complete a task, push beyond obstacles, show discipline and commitment, allow ourselves to make mistakes and learn, or act according to our values and conscience, we gain strength and self-knowledge. Tiny triumphs reinforce the neural pathways of self-efficacy. Progress fosters self-trust and an expanded sense of capability. Our resilience, knowledge-building and willingness to stay the course, however quietly, become our proof of inner merit.

The small wins peppering our days thus provide the raw material for sturdier self-regard and assurance to take on larger challenges. Each unseen victory becomes a brushstroke in the ever-emerging self-portrait of who we are and what we are capable of under the surface. The moments when we prevail over self-doubt and fear, resist temptation, work through confusion, stand up for ourselves or others, make responsible choices, and take creative risks gift us increasing faith in our inner wisdom and power.

The Best Confidence–Builder: Small Wins

In a world full of external markers of success money, fame, status nothing builds unshakable confidence quite like self-efficacy: recognizing through experience our capacity to handle challenges and achieve meaningful outcomes.

No praise or accolade from the outside can match the empowerment that comes from witnessing our own abilities firsthand. As it turns out, one of the most potent ways to foster robust self-efficacy is celebrating the small, everyday victories along our path.

Incremental progress made in pursuit of goals however modest provides tangible proof that we can mobilize inner resources like discipline, determination and courage while learning and expanding limits over time. Each micro-win chips away at self-doubt as we watch ourselves deliberately move the needle forward. We glean direct evidence of being able to endure discomfort, solve problems, creatively respond to obstacles and own our advancement. Savory self-efficacy from life's unseen victories makes us bolder and more motivated to keep pursuing fulfillment. Let's see how.

The Potency of Progress

One of the most empowering gifts of unseen victories is how they nurture self-efficacy our belief in our competence and ability to accomplish goals. Every small win achieved in pursuit of growth feeds our self-perception about what we can handle and overcome. Each micro-achievement becomes a deposit in the confidence bank we draw on to face new challenges.

Seeing Our Own Strength

Pursuing a passion project, learning a new skill, having a health and fitness breakthrough, speaking up for our needs these acts involve courage, discipline, resilience, and expanding limits. When we acknowledge unseen victories within goal striving of any scale, we witness firsthand our grit. We recognize we can endure discomfort to grow and better trust our capacity to show up for objectives that matter.

Owning Our Progress

Similarly, when we pause to honor effort and increments of progress made, we affirm our agency and direction over life. We realize that through our commitment and willingness to learn, we can gradually build competency and mastery. We feel the momentum that comes from praising our small but hard-won steps forward. Our self-efficacy solidifies as we own our advancement.

Overcoming Self-Doubt

Each time we confront fear yet act anyway whether giving a presentation, expressing vulnerability, or tackling a stretch goal we earn a small win and chip away at self-doubt. We internalize, "I can face challenges and succeed," crystallizing boldness. Our sense of what we can accomplish expands.

Trusting Our Abilities

As we reflect on taking risks that paid off creative leaps, handling new responsibilities, persevering through confusion to find solutions we build faith in our abilities. Awareness of how we thoughtfully navigated uncertainty breeds confidence we can respond adequately to novel situations going forward. Our self-trust grows.

Uncovering Hidden Abundance

As these examples illustrate, celebrating unseen victories illuminates undiscovered reserves of strength, courage and competence buried within. What we reference implicitly reminding ourselves, "If others can do this, so can I" - we make real through small wins. Our self-efficacy surfaces one micro-triumph at a time.

Cultivating Self–Worth Through Unseen Victories

Self-worth is a deeply personal quality immune to external modifiers like talent, beauty or material success. It springs from an inner sense of our inherent value. Yet despite being infinitely precious, self-worth often wavers when the outside world fails to validate us or harsh inner critics attacks our worth. The good news is there lies within each of us an unlimited wellspring of value that reveals itself through life's small, courageous efforts.

When we create from passion, stand up for our convictions, care for our wellbeing, extend compassion to others, and allow our authentic truth expression, we strengthen self-worth. By honoring the unassuming ways we positively impact our inner and outer worlds, we cultivate respect for who we are beneath surface judgments. Our small acts of wisdom breed valuation of that wisdom. Our tiny steps toward self-actualization mirror back our preciousness and the sacred right to blossom. Our unseen victories illuminate our deservingness of care and dignity. Let's examine how.

Nurturing Self-Worth Through Quiet Achievements

An incredibly empowering aspect of unseen victories is that they often reflect and reinforce our authentic values and interests. Completing a passion project, making time for self-care, showing compassion toward others, and standing up for beliefs build self-worth by honoring who we genuinely are. When we acknowledge the small wins embedded in self-directed actions, we recognize our core self staring back at us in the mirror. We feel the dignity, respect and validation that comes from choices aligned with inner truth. We see reflected our best self creative, wise and caring.

Learning to Trust Ourselves

As we tune into inner wisdom and set boundaries around rest, creative time, or health needs, we build trust in our instincts. We gain evidence from resulting wellbeing boosts that we merit loyalty. Each small act of self-compassion makes us value our needs and company more fully.

Owning Our Wisdom and Growth

Additionally, when we pause to appreciate effort and small gains made in terms of knowledge, restraint, empathy and insight, we nurture self-worth by honoring our wisdom. We realize through incremental growth that we can increasingly listen to ourselves, trust our inner voice, set healthy boundaries, and compassionately attend to needs our own and others'.

J.K. Rowling's Quiet Achievements

Few stories exemplify the power of unseen victories to build self-worth quite like that of J .K. Rowling. Before becoming a globally renowned author, Rowling found herself jobless, divorced, and struggling through depression as a single parent living on welfare. Her dream of writing novels seemed laughably impossible.

Yet in those darkest hours, Rowling hung onto her passion and kept plugging away at the story rattling around in her head. Writing in cafes after walking her baby to sleep, she slowly assembled the chapters of Harry Potter and the Sorcerer's Stone between desperate moments. Though utterly demoralized, each small achievement of adding prose day-by-day repre-sented an act of self-care amidst adversity.

Just completing her cherished creative work became an unseen victory affirming her perse-verance and identity as a writer. But when publishers unanimously rejected her manu-script, Rowling had to dig deeper. By picking herself up and resubmitting, she honored her talents despite outside denial of her worth. When the book finally sold for a mere £2,500 advance, Rowling celebrated the quiet tri-umph of tenacity over resignation.

In retrospect, Rowling calls that period "rock bottom." Yet those relentless small feats of owning her passion, self-belief and dedication laid foundations of unshakable self-worth. Each unseen victory - writing after exhaustion, risking more rejection - crystallized her self-respect and manifested the woman she aimed to be. As she now reflects, her greatest pride isn't Harry Potter's success but showing her children "you can respect yourself, you fought through it."

Her unseen triumphs, though invisible globally, made her see her formidable character and value even during bleakest eras of self-doubt. So, when fame materialized and billions marveled at J.K. Rowling's imaginative wizardry, her essential self-worth was already securely constructed through years of unheralded, everyday courage and creative integrity.

Glimpsing Wholeness

Ultimately, self-worth dwells in embracing all that we are light and shadow, strength and struggle. Each unseen victory opens a window where we glimpse wholeness. Our small acts of courage while afraid, humility when we fall short, and willingness to make amends and keep growing despite stumbles, allow us to see and make peace with our complex, imperfect yet earnest humanity. Here dwells genuine self-acceptance and regard.

Recognizing Our Own Gold

The Incan people of South America have an ancient saying: "Everything you are seeking is seeking you." The same might be said of self-worth it is already within us, awakened through unseen daily effort.

When we reflect on the trials we have already overcome, knowledge hard-won, values we honor in choices small and large, and caring shown others along life's margins ... we hold all the proof needed of our inherent worth. Like prospectors, we uncover glints of gold courage, creativity, compassion that reveal our preciousness and power if we dare to see.

Through celebrating every small win of learning, progressing, forgiving and standing in truth, self-worth ceases to depend on external verification. As we witness our authenticity in unconscious acts of uncommon valor woven through our days, we glimpse our enduring treasure. For we cannot learn and advance while staying small.

Herein lies the golden opportunity in our many unseen victories: the invitation to know at the deepest levels who we actually are by honoring what we are becoming along the way. Our every small win, failure and grace-filled stumble toward wisdom reassures us we are building character and capability that will never abandon or betray us. We are growing into our greatest allies and protectors. Thus in celebrating the journey of unseen triumphs, we look into a mirror and recognize self-worth looking back as the light in our eyes kindling brightly from within.

Building Self-Compassion Through Micro-Wins

Self-compassion is a powerful and proven way to build emotional resilience, motivation, and wellbeing. Treating ourselves with kindness and understanding in the face of imperfection, rather than criticism, helps us stay motivated on difficult tasks, navigate setbacks, and protect mental health. Yet self-compassion does not always come naturally. Thankfully, celebrating life's many unseen victories provides a pathway to greater self-care.

The small, daily actions we take to pursue growth and purpose however modest offer opportunities to witness our courage, let go of rigid expectations, and appreciate our efforts. Each micro-win of progress, self-care, and perseverance through uncertainty chips away at harsh inner judgment. Slowly, incrementally, we build faith in our core goodness and worth. We watch ourselves expand limits with compassion. We monitor fear give way to maturation. We hold struggles with grace, not condemnation. Thus life's unseen triumphs supply an alchemy for transmuting self-criticism into gentle understanding fueled by care.

Seeing Our Own Strength

When we acknowledge the small daily actions it took to achieve goals or handle challenges whether starting a intimidating project, acting despite anxiety, or demonstrating a new skill we witness our courage and competence firsthand. We recognize we can endure discomfort to grow. Seeing our own grit this way builds self-compassion.

Celebrating Effort Over Outcomes

Similarly, when we celebrate effort and focus on progress made rather than demanding specific results, we practice self-compassion. We understand growth happens incrementally, that learning means making mistakes. We appreciate our dedication along the uncertain path. Praising our willingness builds care for our process.

Owning Imperfection

Self-compassion also comes from embracing our setbacks, gaps in knowledge or clumsy social moments with humor and grace rather than criticism. By celebrating the unseen victory of simply trying and acknowledging areas for growth, we release judgment and access self-acceptance.

Valuing Our Resilience

Likewise, reflecting on how we summon strength repeatedly in the face of challenges, heal after losses, and renew purpose when plans crumble or dreams fade builds compassion for our elastic inner resources. We suffer setbacks yet bounce back wiser. Appreciating this resilience instills care.

Conclusion

Taking notice of our daily small wins helps give rise to self-compassion. Seeing our own determination, courage, and willingness to learn instills confidence in ourselves.

When we observe our efforts paying off bit by bit - facing a fear, committing to a project, or trying again after a setback - we better appreciate the journey. We witness that progress unfolds slowly if we persist. Struggles teach rather than diminish us. Each learning opportunity and attempt to contribute makes us wiser and more caring overall.

Celebrating these micro-victories means celebrating inherent goodness within ourselves and others. For we all stumble yet get back up, make regrettable choices yet redeem the future, feel insecure yet press on toward dreams. By honoring the resilience and daring involved our own small steps forward, judgment gives way to humble understanding.

Thus pausing to notice modest gains or attempts offers a path to self-care. Here we catch ourselves showing compassion by enduring discomfort for growth, taking risks, and forgiving missteps. We find cause to walk gently with ourselves and lend a hand to fellow strugglers. For life invites us to build something beautiful slowly but surely through unsung daily effort. When we celebrate the journey of micro-wins, we discover caring and capability awaiting within.

Fostering Growth And Learning

SOME OF LIFE'S MOST empowering moments come when we realize we have expanded beyond who we were developing new skills, gaining wisdom from mistakes, cultivating strengths like discipline or leadership through small daily efforts.

Yet because the process of growth often happens gradually through modest steps we dismiss, we frequently underestimate our evolution. We fail to honor the learning, emotional maturation and character development happening through our many "unseen victories."

Here we look into how celebrating life's small wins and increments of progress magnifies their growth potential. Appreciating effort and attempts made to stretch oneselflays neural pathways of courage, curiosity and self-efficacy priming further achievement. Reveling in minor milestones fuels motivation and the willingness to stay the often uncomfortable course of increasing mastery, capability and purpose.

Our many micro-wins of conquered inertia, perseverance when frustrated, creative problem solving and building skills brick-by-layer thus supply the very raw material for becoming our best, most contributive selves over time. Let's explore how praising small victories cultivates largescale growth.

Sparking Curiosity Through Small Wins

An empowering aspect of unseen victories is that they build curiosity and engagement. When we pause to acknowledge effort invested and small gains made toward a goal - whether learning part of a language, developing artistic skills or expanding technological literacy momentum builds to continue growing. Celebrating incremental progress renews interest to keep showing up.

Confidence to Explore

Likewise, reflecting on risks outside our comfort zone that paid off, or unfamiliar situations we eventually navigated with success, strengthens confidence to try new things. Recalling how we turned initial confusion into understanding breeds willingness to explore unfamiliar terrain and self-assure we will find our footing. Past micro-wins make curiosity feel safer.

Curiosity as Gateway

Additionally, unseen victories centered on acquiring new knowledge frequently spur new lines of inquiry. & admired innovator Elon Musk has noted, "There is a tremendous bias against asking questions, but asking questions is where you get answers." Each insight uncovered surfaces novel questions, driving discovery.

Stevejobs' Path

Legendary Apple founder Steve Jobs exemplified lifelong curiosity to invent the future. But his innovations rested on micro-wins learning calligraphy skills with no obvious application yet later used for Mac fonts, studying Eastern spirituality before applying Zen design principles. By relentlessly exploring new domains through invisible victories, he revolutionized consumer technology.

Fanning Small Sparks

When we follow curiosity where it leads through modest daily research Each or experimentation, glorious unseen victories of creativity, meaning and capability await discovery. By mining the micro-wins of attempts made out of interest regardless of outcomes, our evolution gains richness and wonder. Thus small sparks of incremental learning nurture sweeping positive change from the inside out when fanned.

Building Skills By Conquering Small Challenges

An essential way unseen victories drive growth is by incrementally developing new skills and abilities. As we break larger goals into mini-objectives and celebrate effort and micro-wins, we reinforce neural pathways of competence while tackling new challenges requires learning. Each small success primes us to perform better next time. Our skills strengthen.

Confidence to Persist

Additionally, when we note the small daily actions that contribute to overcoming obstacles- seeking resources, problem-solving workarounds, digging deeper to find motivation when frustrated - we build faith in our ability to persist through difficulty. We bank evidence we can handle setbacks and invent creative solutions, powering greater resilience.

From Novice to Master

Mark Twain once advised, "Take your first step as soon as possible." Each small step forward lays a brick in rising skill mastery. As leaders and experts from Bruce Lee to Elon Musk attest, replicating simple fundamentals while adding slight lessons over time compounds into excellence. By celebrating the micro-wins along this subtle but seismic path of deep practice, motivation stays strong.

Thus within each small challenge confronted, attempt made and lesson integrated dwells opportunity for immense yet underestimated growth. When we pivot focus from distant peaks to appreciate the terrain traveled so far, transformation unfolds one hard-won victory stride at a time.

Leveraging Unseen Victories to Maximize Learning

Part of strategic growth comes from reviewing efforts made and noting lessons within both successes and failures. Unseen victories provide built-in feedback for fueling improvement if mined. When we stretch to gain new knowledge or attempt an unfamiliar skill, the micro-wins and stumbles encountered supply intuitive data on effective strategies to amplify and potholes to avoid. Each attempt offers tailored input for advancing learning. Tracking this makes progress exponential.

Lessons From the Inside Out

Additionally, because unseen victories often center on inner achievements like overcoming fears, controlling reactions or demonstrating values, they provide especially illuminating self-insight. By regarding how we summon courage, navigate disputes thoughtfully or handle disappointment with grace, we recognize burgeoning wisdom. Our small daily growth mirrors rising emotional intelligence to deploy.

Extracting Insights from Errors

Scientists find that noting lessons within failed attempts, when framed as growth opportunities rather than self-criticism, breeds creative adaptability and innovation. Autopsies of difficulties faced activates parts of the prefrontal cortex associated with cognitive flexibility and openness to change. Error mining unlocks unconventional progress.

Thomas Edison's Grit

Legendary American inventor Thomas Edison, who amassed over 1,000 patents, famously quipped, "I haven't failed. I've just found 10,000 ways that won't work." By celebrating effort and analyzing missteps leading to his phonograph and practical lightbulb, seeming defeats became wisdom breakthroughs.

My Journey of Transformation

My journey is a testament to the power of perseverance and the refusal to surrender to adversity. There was a time when I found myself at a crossroads, my dreams of pursuing higher education and personal growth seemingly out of reach. The weight of societal expectations and self-doubt threatened to extinguish the flame of my ambitions.

However, I refused to succumb to the temptation of giving up. Instead, I tapped into an innate well of resilience and determination, fueled by an unwavering belief in my own capabilities. With each obstacle that presented itself, I responded with a renewed sense of purpose, transforming challenges into stepping stones towards my ultimate goals.

Today, I stand as an example of what can be achieved when one refuses to surrender. I have not only attained remarkable academic achievements, including a bachelor's degree in information technology, a master's in Cybersecurity with honors, and my ongoing pursuit of a Ph.D., but I have also carved out a remarkable career as a leader and visionary.

Through my inspirational book, "7 Ways to Overcome Fear," and my role as the CEO of Ultimate Web Design, I have empowered countless individuals to embrace their true potential. As a lifelong learner, mentor, and inspirational speaker, I guide men and women through the complexities of personal growth, helping them navigate difficult challenges, make informed decisions, and discover their true purpose.

My story is a testament to the transformative power of resilience and the unwavering pursuit of one's dreams. By refusing to give up, I have not only transformed my own life but have become a beacon of hope and inspiration for others, reminding them that their greatest triumphs often lie on the other side of their greatest challenges.

Owning the Journey

Furthermore, when we purposefully appreciate effort invested and skills sharpened through repetition and mistakes made, we own our learning rather than judging imperfect results. We realize mastery comes slowly but assuredly through compound practice. We observe that missteps teach untold lessons if studied without shame. Each incremental gain becomes a jewel of progress celebrating rather than critiquing our journey.

Mental Benefits of Tracking Progress

In multiple studies, people who monitored small progress daily felt 7% more capable of achieving their goals and 19% more motivated over 2 months compared to non-trackers. Progress visibility inspires perseverance.

Researchers find that employees who consciously tally and collect examples of their successful efforts are 13% more engaged and productive in their workplace roles. Progress tracking catalyzes effectiveness.

Emotional Upsides of Reflection

People who take just 60-90 seconds after completing tasks to write about lessons learned demonstrate heightened creativity and 23% stronger memory in applying those insights to future projects.

Reflection potentiates learning.

Scientists observe that celebrating incremental improvement on meaningful quests lights up neural regions tied to positive emotions like pride and satisfaction while reducing zones linked to fear. Small wins feel monumental to the brain.

Overcoming Obstacles through Micro-Resilience

Studies reveal that viewing adversity as isolated setbacks rather than personal defects predicts faster rebound from challenges. Framing obstacles through a growth mindset lens empowers comeback.

The Compounding Value of Deliberate Practice

Multiple assessments of top experts demonstrate that logging 10,000+ hours of purposeful skills repetition to continually refine fundamentals explains the rise from novices to elite status. But the journey unfolds through building micro-capabilities step-by-step. Unseen daily victories stack up to supremacy.

Conclusion

In a culture fixated on overnight success and instant gratification, the real driver of sustained excellence and empowerment lives camouflaged in plain sight the untold number of micro-wins achieved through simple persistence. Behind storied careers, relationships that endure, innovations shaping the horizon line and wisdom acquired to uplift humanity ... resides an accumulation of small, courageous, often agonizing steps in defiance of doubt, fatigue and convenience.

Yet dwelling within our willingness to rise again when plans crumble, creatively adapt around obstacles, take baby steps to expand our limits and integrate the lessons revealed through stumbling forward hides the genuine substance of leaders, creators and change-makers. Each micro-win weights the scale incrementally toward the person capable of improving both inner and outer worlds because they built faith in their voice and convictions.

As this chapter explored, by taking pause to notice and celebrate the invisible victories through which we gradually level up skills, emotional aptitude, problems solving and character ... we stoke momentum toward realizing potential and purpose. For in the end, our human glory rides not on some illusive grand finale but rather on the courage and care applied to progressing day-by-day. ur many unseen victories light the path home to our best self and finest hour.

# The Value of Small Wins

LET'S LEARN THE IMPORTANCE of recognizing the value of small wins in your life. Learn how they contribute to your overall well-being. Acknowledging and celebrating these seemingly insignificant achievements can boost your self-esteem and motivation, ultimately leading to more tremendous success in your personal and professional endeavors.

Embrace the Journey

Life's journey is filled with numerous destinations, but the path to each milestone is equally important. Embracing the journey means appreciating every step, not just the final achievement. It's about understanding that each challenge and setback is a part of the growth process.

By focusing on the journey, we learn resilience, adaptability, and the true value of perseverance. This perspective encourages us to find meaning and joy in the progress we make every day, rather than waiting to reach a distant goal to feel fulfilled.

Thinks of it as a to-do list. You focus on small tasks that fill your list and by accomplishing those tasks, you complete your list.

Joy in Success

Small moments of success are often over-looked, yet they are the very essence of joy in our daily lives. Celebrating these moments encourages a positive outlook and nurtures our emotional well-being. It's about finding happiness in progress, no matter how minor it may seem. This practice helps to build a foundation of contentment and motivation, driving us forward with a sense of achievement and purpose. By valuing these little moments, we cultivate a life filled with joy and satisfaction.

Honor the Effort

Every small win is a testament to effort, dedication, and perseverance. Recognizing the hard work behind each achievement reinforces the importance of persistence and resilience. It's not just about the outcome but the journey and effort it takes to get there. This acknowledgment fosters a sense of pride and accomplishment, encouraging us to keep striving towards our goals. Honoring the effort helps to build a strong work ethic and a resilient spirit, essential for long-term success.

Focus on Daily Wins

Shifting focus from overarching goals to daily accomplishments allows us to celebrate our progress and maintain motivation. This approach breaks down daunting tasks into manageable steps, making goals more attainable. By recognizing daily wins, we stay engaged and proactive, keeping the momentum going. This strategy not only helps in achieving long-term objectives but also enhances our sense of satisfaction and fulfillment in our everyday lives.

Gratitude for Victories

Cultivating a mindset of gratitude for small victories enriches our lives with positivity and appreciation. Acknowledging even the smallest successes makes us more mindful of our progress and blessings. This gratitude elevates our mood, improves mental health, and strengthens our resilience against challenges. By valuing each small victory, we foster a positive outlook that propels us forward with hope and determination.

Motivation from Wins

Small wins are powerful motivators that fuel our drive for future success. Each achievement, no matter how minor, builds confidence and momentum, pushing us closer to our goals.

Recognizing and celebrating these wins enhances our motivation, making daunting tasks feel more achievable. This cycle of success and motivation creates a positive feedback loop, where each small win propels us towards greater achievements.

Impact of Progress

Consistent progress, marked by small wins, accumulates over time to yield significant impact. This approach emphasizes the power of persistence and gradual improvement. By valuing each step forward, we recognize the transformative power of consistent effort. This perspective shifts our focus from instant gratification to long-term growth, highlighting the profound impact of sustained progress.

Value in Growth

Personal growth and development stem from the accumulation of small achievements. Each small step forward contributes to our overall growth, shaping us into more capable, resilient individuals. Valuing these achievements encourages a mindset of continuous improvement and self-reflection. It's a reminder that personal development is an ongoing process, enriched by every small success along the way.

Empowerment through Acknowledgment

Acknowledging small steps towards success is empowering. It reaffirms our capability to achieve our goals and boosts our self-esteem. This acknowledgment serves as a reminder of our potential and progress, motivating us to continue our efforts. By celebrating these small steps, we not only recognize our achievements but also empower ourselves to tackle future challenges with confidence.

Conclusion

In life, it is easy to become fixated on the end goal, the destination that we are striving towards. However, true fulfillment comes from embracing the journey itself, not just the final outcome. Each step along the way, each small achievement, is a victory in its own right. By acknowledging and celebrating these small wins, we can find joy in the process of reaching our goals.It is important to find joy in the little moments of success, no matter how insignificant they may seem. Every accomplishment, no matter how small, is a step in the right direction. By honoring the effort behind every small win, we can appreciate the hard work and dedication that goes into achieving our goals.

Instead of focusing solely on big, overarching goals, we can shift our attention to daily accomplishments. By setting small, achievable milestones for ourselves, we can track our progress and celebrate each step forward. Cultivating a mindset of gratitude for these small victories allows us to stay motivated and focused on the journey ahead. Harnessing the motivation of small wins can fuel future success.

By recognizing the impact of consistent progress over time, we can see how each small achievement adds up to something greater. Valuing personal growth and development through these small accomplishments empowers us to reach our full potential. By acknowledging and celebrating the small steps we take towards success, we can empower ourselves to keep pushing forward. Each small achievement is a victory in itself, and by honoring these moments, we can cultivate a mindset of positivity and gratitude. In this way, we can find joy in the journey and fuel our motivation for future success.

The Ripple Effect of Positivity

POSITIVITY AND SMALL ACHIEVE-MENTS have profound impact of in our lives. Through the concept of the "Ripple Effect of Positivity," here we discuss how even the smallest victories and acts of self-appreciation can have far-reaching consequences that extend beyond ourselves. By cultivating a mindset of gratitude and celebrating our own milestones, we not only boost our own confidence and self-worth, but also inspire those around us to

do the same. Once you recognize the significance of your own achievements, no matter
how small, you'll appreciate the ripple effect
they can have on your own life and the lives of
others. It will also equip you with the tools to
create a positive feedback loop of self-appreciation and empowerment, leading to a more
fulfilling and impactful existence.

Positive Thinking

Embracing positive thinking transforms challenges into opportunities for growth. This
mindset not only improves personal well-being but also influences those around us. By focusing on positive thoughts, we enhance our
resilience, creativity, and ability to solve problems. This proactive approach to life encourages a more fulfilling and productive lifestyle,

demonstrating that our thoughts have the power to shape our reality.

Culture of Support

Cultivating a culture of encouragement and support within our communities and relationships fosters an environment where everyone can thrive. This culture is built on mutual respect, understanding, and genuine care for others' well-being. By lifting others, we not only contribute to their success but also create a network of support that we can rely on. Encouragement acts as a catalyst for confidence and growth, making it a cornerstone for positive communal relationships.

Kindness Impact

Small acts of kindness carry a significant impact, creating waves of positivity that extend far beyond the initial gesture. Recognizing the power of these acts encourages us to engage in kindness daily. Whether it's a simple smile, a helping hand, or a thoughtful word, these gestures can brighten someone's day, improve relationships, and contribute to a more compassionate society. The cumulative effect of kindness fosters a sense of community and belonging.

Joy in Compliments

Spreading joy through genuine compliments is a simple yet profound way to uplift others. Compliments acknowledge the value and efforts of those around us, boosting their morale and self-esteem. This exchange of positive energy not only strengthens relationships but also encourages a culture of appreciation and positivity. By making an effort to notice and vocalize the good in others, we contribute to a more supportive and encouraging environment.

Self-Appreciation

Nurturing self-appreciation is crucial for lasting personal change and well-being. Recognizing our own worth and accomplishments fosters self-love, confidence, and resilience. This self-recognition motivates us to pursue our goals and face challenges with a positive outlook. By valuing ourselves, we set a foundation for growth and happiness, showing that self-appreciation is not just self-care but a necessity for a fulfilling life.

Resilience and Positivity

Building resilience through a positive mindset equips us to navigate life's ups and downs more effectively. A resilient spirit, fostered by optimism, helps us to recover from setbacks and maintain our focus on personal growth and goals. This mindset encourages us to see failures as learning opportunities and challenges as chances to improve, enhancing our ability to adapt and thrive in various circumstances.

Optimism for Growth

Harnessing the power of optimism is essential for personal development. An optimistic outlook inspires us to pursue our aspirations with confidence and determination. It drives us to seek solutions and opportunities even in adversity, promoting continuous growth and learning. By adopting an optimistic attitude, we open ourselves to new possibilities and paths to success, demonstrating that optimism is a key component of personal and professional development.

Community Positivity

Creating a ripple effect of positivity in our community starts with individual actions. By embodying positive behaviors and attitudes, we inspire others to do the same, leading to a collective uplift in community spirit. This ripple effect enhances social connections, fosters mutual support, and builds a more cohesive and resilient community. Engaging in community initiatives and spreading positivity not only enriches our lives but also strengthens the fabric of our society.

Focusing on the Good

Shifting perspectives to focus on the good in life encourages a more hopeful and content outlook. This shift in focus highlights the beauty and potential in our surroundings and experiences, mitigating the impact of negativity and challenges. By choosing to see the positive aspects of our lives, we cultivate a sense of gratitude and happiness, which contributes to our overall well-being and satisfaction.

Everyday Victories

Celebrating the beauty of everyday victories recognizes the significance of small achievements and moments of joy. These celebrations nurture a sense of accomplishment and gratitude, reinforcing a positive outlook on life. By valuing these daily wins, we acknowledge our progress and the simple pleasures that make life fulfilling. This practice encourages us to appreciate the present and find happiness in the journey, not just in the destination.

Conclusion

Embrace the power of positive thinking as a foundational principle for personal growth and success. By shifting your mindset towards optimism and focusing on the good in every situation, you can cultivate a sense of resilience that helps them overcome challenges and setbacks. This positive mindset not only benefits you but also creates a ripple effect of positivity in your immediate community, spreading joy and encouragement to those around you. One of the key ways to foster a culture of positivity is through cultivating a spirit of encouragement and support.

By recognizing the impact of small acts of kindness and spreading joy through genuine compliments, you can create a nurturing environment that uplifts and empowers others.

These small gestures of kindness not only brighten someone's day, but also contribute to a sense of collective well-being and community spirit. This importance of self-appreciation for lasting change is the central message of Unseen Victories.

When you nurture a sense of self-worth and celebrating the beauty of everyday victories, you can build a foundation of confidence and resilience. It will empower you to achieve your goals and dreams. Through recognizing and celebrating their own achievements, one can cultivate a positive mindset that enables them to overcome obstacles and thrive in the face of adversity.

Harness the power of optimism and shift your perspectives to focus on the good. This will help you create a ripple effect of positivity that can transforms not only your own lives, but also the lives of those around you. Through small acts of kindness, genuine compliments, and a spirit of encouragement and support, once can spread joy and create a culture of positivity all around. Ultimately, by celebrating the beauty of everyday victories and nurturing self-appreciation, you can build resilience and bring about personal growth.

Cultivating a Growth Mindset

WHAT IS THE IMPORTANCE of cultivating a growth mindset? Well, it can help you overcome challenges with resilience and determination. Here, we check the concept of viewing setbacks as opportunities for growth and learning, rather than insurmountable obstacles. You start taking your success as a marathon, not a sprint. You change your mindset and the life changes for you.

By adopting a growth mindset, you can persevere in the face of adversity and continue with your determination to push forward. By embracing a growth mindset, you will be better prepared to overcome challenges and achieve unseen victories in your own life. Preparation is evetything. Be it cooking a meal, or facing challenges.

Small is Big

Think of evety little success as a big deal. It's like giving yourself a high five every time you move a step closer to your goal. This keeps you pumped and reminds you that you're doing great, even if the finish line seems far away. It's all about seeing the good in the effort you're putting in.

Focus on Progress

Instead of just looking at the final goal, pay attention to how far you've come. Every step forward is progress, and that's what really matters. This way, when things get tough, you remember you're moving forward, and that's a win. It's like cheering yourself on, knowing every little bit of progress counts.

Appreciate Yourself

Give yourself some credit! Recognize how awesome you are for trying, succeeding, and even just sticking with it. This self-pat on the back boosts your confidence, making you feel ready to take on the world. It's about seeing your worth and believing in your power to do great things. And, after all, you are your best friend!

So, take time everyday to appreciate your efforts, celebrate your small wins!

Personal Growth Celebration

Celebrate your growth journey. It's not just about the big wins but also about the steps you've taken to improve yourself. Acknowledging your growth makes you appreciate the journey and keeps you motivated to keep going. It's like throwing a party for your progress, no matter how big or small.

Embrace Challenge Journeys

Look at challenges as adventures. They're not there to stop you but to make you stronger and wiser. Facing them with courage turns these hurdles into stepping stones. It's like going on a treasure hunt where every challenge is a clue to finding your strength.

Strength in Resilience

Being resilient and determined is your super-power. It means bouncing back from tough times and not giving up on what you want. It's about standing strong in the face of challenges and knowing that you've got what it takes to push through.

Power of Positivity

Stay positive. It's about focusing on what you can do and finding the silver lining in tough situations. This positive vibe helps you find solutions and keeps you hopeful. It's like having a sunshine mindset, even on cloudy days.

Perseverance and Grit

Keep pushing, no matter what. Grit is all about not throwing in the towel, even when things get really hard. It's the toughness that keeps you going, believing in your dreams, and knowing that you'll get there with enough effort and patience.

Continuous Improvement

Always aim to get better. It's about loving to learn, being open to feedback, and always looking for ways to improve. This mindset keeps you growing and adapting, making sure you're always moving forward. It's like being on a never-ending quest to be your best self.

Conclusion

In our fast-paced and results-driven world, it can be easy to overlook the significance of small victories. However, recognizing and celebrating these accomplishments is essential for building self-esteem and motivation. Whether it's completing a task ahead of schedule or making progress towards a goal, every small win contributes to our overall success and well-being. By acknowledging these achievements, we can boost our confidence and momentum, ultimately leading to greater accomplishments in the long run. Instead of solely focusing on the end result, we should shift our attention to the progress we make along the way. By setting smaller milestones and tracking our development, we can stay motivated and engaged in our pursuits. This shift in mindset allows us to appreciate the journey and the growth that comes with it, rather than fixating on the final outcome. In doing so, we can cultivate a sense of fulfilment and satisfaction in our efforts, regardless of the end result. Self-appreciation plays a crucial role in building confidence and resilience. By recognizing our strengths, achievements, and progress, we can boost our self-esteem and belief in our abilities. Celebrating personal growth and development, no matter how small, reinforces a positive self-image and encourages us to continue striving for excellence.

Through self-appreciation, we can cultivate a strong sense of self-worth and confidence that empowers us to overcome challenges and obstacles. The journey of personal growth is filled with challenges and setbacks, but it is through overcoming these obstacles that we find strength and resilience. By embracing these challenges as opportunities for growth and learning, we can develop the perseverance and determination needed to succeed. With a mindset focused on resilience and determination, we can navigate through adversity with grace and resilience, emerging stronger and more capable than before. Positive thinking is a powerful tool that can help us overcome obstacles and achieve our goals. By harnessing the power of positive thinking, we can shift our mindset from one of doubt and fear to one of optimism and possibility.

Cultivating a positive outlook allows us to approach challenges with a sense of hope and confidence, enabling us to persevere in the face of adversity. By maintaining a positive attitude, we can cultivate a mindset of perseverance and grit that propels us towards success. Continuous improvement and learning are essential components of personal growth and development. By fostering a culture of continuous improvement, we can strive for excellence and push ourselves to reach new heights. Embracing a mindset of constant learning and growth allows us to adapt to change, overcome challenges, and achieve our full potential. By seeking out new opportunities for growth and development, we can continuously evolve and improve, both personally and professionally.

How To Recognize Your Unseen Victories?

AS WE'VE DISCUSSED so far, unseen victories represent the parade of modest but monumental daily wins, acts of progress, and evidence of wisdom and strength shepherding us toward realizing higher purpose.

From overcoming fears and resistance, to stretching skills, demonstrating values consistency, and amplifying empathy and balance through simple, humble choices ... we sculpt remarkable lives with grit and grace beyond the spotlight.

Yet to reap the profound emotional, psychological and personal development dividends unlocked by unseen victories, we must attune ourselves to notice the victories hiding in plain sight.

Appreciating and honoring the hard-earned milestones and lessons embedded in daily work plays a strategic role in goal achievement and cultivating self-worth. But unless we adjust focus to process our tiny triumphs as they occur, their gifts are lost like dust in the wind.

This chapter guides you through a practical four-step toolkit for intentionally recognizing the unseen victories tangled in your daily activities and growth efforts.

Curating habits of acknowledging wins, progress, setbacks overcome, self-discoveries and values courage tethers your attention to the triumph narrative unfolding through gritty mental rehearsal and tiny, conscious decisions fueling your emergence. You are already the hero of countless unseen victories deserving recognition ... now let's ensure you collect their gold!

Tips and strategies to identify your unseen victories

Setting Realistic and Specific Goals

Strategy: Instead of aiming for overly ambitious or vague objectives, set achievable, clear goals that can be easily tracked. This makes it easier to recognize when you've reached a milestone, no matter how small.

Example: Instead of setting a goal to "get fit," aim for specific targets like "jog for 20 minutes three times a week" or "attend two yoga classes per week." This way, you can easily see your progress and celebrate when you meet these smaller, specific goals.

Tracking Your Progress

Strategy: Keep a journal, use an app, or maintain a spreadsheet to record your daily achievements. Seeing your progress written down can make it more tangible and rewarding.

Example: If your goal is to write a book, track the number of words or pages you write each day. Even on days when it feels like you haven't done much, seeing the cumulative effect of your efforts can be a victory in itself.

Reviewing Your Accomplishments Regularly

Strategy: Set aside time weekly or monthly to review what you've achieved. This can help you see how small achievements accumulate over time and are worth celebrating.

Example: At the end of each month, review your tracked progress towards learning a new language. Celebrate milestones like completing a set of lessons or having a basic conversation. Recognizing these moments can boost your morale and motivation.

Setting Personal Rewards

Strategy: Associate small rewards with reaching your goals or milestones. This creates a positive reinforcement loop, making the journey more enjoyable and motivating.

Example: If your goal is to declutter your home, reward yourself with a relaxing bath or an episode of your favorite show after organizing each room. These rewards make the process satisfying and highlight the victory in completing each task.

Sharing Your Achievements

Strategy: Share your progress and victories, no matter how small, with friends or family members. Sometimes, others can help us see the value in what we've accomplished when we might overlook it.

Example: If you've managed to save money by cooking at home for a week, share this achievement with a friend. Their recognition and encouragement can serve as an additional reward, highlighting the victory in your discipline and effort.

Reflecting on Personal Growth

Strategy: Take time to reflect on how each small victory contributes to your personal growth. Understanding the bigger picture can help you appreciate the significance of small wins.

Example: Reflect on how overcoming your fear of public speaking through small steps, like speaking up during meetings, has improved your confidence and professional presence. Recognizing this growth as a series of victories can be incredibly rewarding.

To spot and cheer for the "Unseen Victories" in our lives, it's all about keeping things simple and positive. First off, make sure the goals you set are clear and doable it's like setting yourself up to win right from the start. Keeping track of what you're doing and how far you've come is super important too. It's like having a map that shows you're on the right path and encourages you to keep going.

Don't forget to give yourself a pat on the back for the small stuff. It's those little wins that keep our spirits high. Every now and then, take a moment to look back at what you've done. You'll often be surprised at how much you've achieved. Talking to friends or family about your journey can also give you a fresh perspective. They might see successes that you didn't even realize were a big deal. And if things don't go as planned, that's okay too. It's all part of the process. Instead of getting down about it, try to see what you can learn from it. Every attempt, whether it works out or not, teaches us something and gets us closer to where we want to be.

So, in a nutshell, finding and appreciating those "Unseen Victories" is about setting realistic goals, keeping an eye on your progress, celebrating the small wins, reviewing how far you've come, getting feedback, and learning from the bumps along the way. It's about enjoying the journey, with all its ups and downs, and knowing that every step forward is a win in its own right.

Do it in your daily life

In the hustle of everyday life, it's easy to overlook the small accomplishments and victories that pave the way to our larger goals. However, making a conscious effort to recognize these "Unseen Victories" can significantly impact our happiness, motivation, and resilience. Here's how you can make this practice a part of your daily routine, along with real-life examples to inspire you.

Make it a Daily Habit

Set aside a few minutes at the end of each day to reflect on what you've accomplished. This could be as simple as writing down three things you're proud of from your day. They don't have to be groundbreaking achievements; often, it's the small steps that count the most. This daily practice turns your attention to the positive, helping to cultivate a mindset of growth and appreciation.

Example: Perhaps you managed to drink eight glasses of water throughout the day, stayed patient during a stressful situation at work, or finally started on a project you've been postponing. These are all victories worth acknowledging.

Share Your Successes

Talking about your successes with friends or family members can amplify the feeling of accomplishment. It also allows you to share joy and encourages a culture of recognition and positivity among your loved ones. Example: If you've been working on becoming more organized and you managed to keep your workspace clean for a week, share this with a friend. This might seem small, but it's a step towards a larger goal of organization and productivity.

Set Weekly Reflections

Beyond daily acknowledgments, consider a deeper reflection once a week. Look back over the week and identify moments where you were particularly resilient, where you made progress on your goals, or where you learned something new.

Example: Maybe you faced a challenging task at work and, through research and asking for help, you were able to overcome it. This not only shows progress in your project but also in your problem-solving and communication skills. When you pay attention to such victories, your brain maps these victories as solid foundations.

Celebrate the "Unseen"

Celebrating these victories, no matter how small, reinforces the behavior and mindset that led to those successes. It could be as simple as treating yourself to a favorite meal, taking a day off for self-care, or just giving yourself a moment to feel proud.

Example: After consistently practicing a new skill-like cooking or a new language-for a month, celebrate by sharing your new skill with friends or rewarding yourself with something that enhances this new hobby, like a new cookbook or language learning app.

Learn from Every Outcome

Sometimes, our unseen victories are hidden within the lessons we learn from setbacks. Reflecting on what didn't go as planned and identifying what you learned from the experience is a victory in itself.

Example: If you attempted a new recipe and it didn't turn out as expected, the effort you put into trying something new and the lessons learned for next time are victories worth celebrating.

Encourage Others

Finally, recognizing and celebrating the unseen victories of those around you can create a ripple effect of positivity. By acknowledging the efforts and progress of others, you not only boost their morale but also encourage a culture of appreciation and support.

Example: Notice when a colleague takes the initiative on a difficult project or when a family member makes an effort to improve a skill. A simple acknowledgment can go a long way in reinforcing their positive actions. Everyone likes appreciation. A few encouraging words from you can uplift their spirits, spread positivity all around, which will finally lighten up your world.

Conclusion

Regularly recognizing your unseen victories is a powerful practice that can transform your perspective, boost your morale, and encourage continuous growth. By making this practice a habit, you'll start to notice more joy in the journey towards your goals, appreciate the learning in every setback, and foster an environment of positivity and support both for

yourself and those around you. Let's start celebrating our unseen victories today and every
day.

Sharing Your Unseen Victories With Others

YOU KNOW THOSE LITTLE wins you get throughout your day? The stuff that makes you quietly proud but doesn't always get a trophy or a round of applause?

This chapter is all about those moments the unseen victories. But here's the twist: we're going to talk about how to share these wins with others.

It might feel a bit weird at first, like you're brag-ging about the small stuff, but that's not it at all. Sharing these moments is about spreading positivity, connecting with people, and maybe even inspiring someone else along the way.

Think of it this way: when you share a little win, you're not just saying, "Hey, look at me!" You're saying, "Hey, if I can do it, so can you." It's about making those invisible wins visible, not just for you, but for everyone around you.

This chapter will guide you through the simple ways you can start doing this. We'll cover why it's a good idea to share your wins, how it can make you and the people around you feel good, and how it can turn into a habit that re-ally makes a difference in your life and others'.

We're going to keep it super straightforward, with real-life examples and easy tips you can start using right away. Whether it's a small victory like finally organizing your desk or something bigger like overcoming a fear, we'll show you how to share these moments in a way that feels natural and genuine. By the end of this chapter, you'll see how sharing your unseen victories can bring you closer to people, boost your confidence, and create an environment where everyone feels a little more appreciated and a lot more connected. Let's dive in and learn how to celebrate the small stuff together.

Tips and Strategies: How To Share Your Unseen Victories with Others

Sharing your unseen victories is a powerful way to connect with others, inspire, and create a positive environment around you. Here are six tips and strategies to help you share these moments effectively and authentically.

Choose Supportive and Positive People

Find Your Cheerleaders: Share your victories with friends, family, or colleagues who are known for their supportive and positive nature. These people are your cheerleaders; they genuinely want to see you succeed and will celebrate your achievements with you, no matter how small. This creates a safe and encouraging space for sharing.

Be Honest and Humble

Keep it Real: When sharing your victories, honesty and humility go a long way. It's not about boasting but about sharing a part of your journey. Talk about the challenges you faced along the way and how you overcame them. This approach not only makes your story more relatable but also more inspiring.

Incorporate Storytelling

Share the Story, Not Just the Victory: People connect with stories more than facts. When you share your unseen victory, tell the story behind it. What led to this win? What obstacles did you face? How did you feel? A good story can turn a small victory into an inspiring tale of perseverance and determination.

Ask for Feedback and Advice

Engage in Meaningful Conversations: After sharing your victory, engage your listener by asking for feedback or advice on your next steps. This not only shows that you value their opinion but also deepens the connection by involving them in your journey. It can also provide you with valuable insights for future endeavors.

Celebrate Others' Victories Too

Make it a Two-Way Street: Sharing isn't just about talking; it's also about listening. Make sure to celebrate the victories of others as enthusiastically as you share your own. This creates a culture of mutual appreciation and encouragement, making it easier for everyone to share and celebrate their unseen victories.

Use Social Media Wisely

Share with a Broader Audience: Social media can be a powerful tool for sharing your victories with a wider audience. However, it's important to use it wisely. Share stories that you think can motivate or inspire others. Remember to stay humble and genuine, and always aim to create a positive impact with your posts.

Conclusion:

Sharing your unseen victories can be incredibly rewarding, not just for you but for those around you. It's a way to spread positivity, inspire others, and strengthen your connections. By choosing the right people, being honest and humble, telling your story, engaging in meaningful conversations, celebrating others, and using social media wisely, you can share your achievements in a way that feels genuine and impactful. Let's embrace the power of sharing our victories, no matter how small they may seem.

How to apply these tips and strategies in different situations?

Let's dive into practical examples of how you can apply these tips and strategies to share your unseen victories in various situations. These examples will help illustrate how to bring these concepts to life in your daily interactions.

Sharing with a Close Friend

Choose Supportive and Positive People: Imagine you've finally managed to stick to a healthy eating habit for a month. You decide to share this victory with a close friend who's always encouraged your efforts to live healthily.

Over coffee, you tell them about your journey, the challenges of resisting cravings, and how you've managed to overcome them. Your friend, being supportive, celebrates your achievement and suggests a healthy recipe you could try next.

During a Work Meeting

Be Honest and Humble: You've completed a project under budget and ahead of schedule. In your next team meeting, you share this victory but also highlight the team's effort and the challenges you faced together.

You acknowledge everyone's hard work and express gratitude for their support, making the victory a collective achievement rather than just your own.

Networking Events

Incorporate Storytelling: At a networking event, you're discussing your career journey with peers. When sharing your unseen victory of learning a new software on your own, you weave a story around it - the initial struggle, the late nights spent on tutorials, and the satisfaction of finally mastering it.

This story sparks a conversation on self-learning, leading to a deeper exchange of experiences and tips.

Asking for Feedback

Ask for Feedback and Advice: After successfully organizing a communiry cleanup, you share the outcome with a mentor, focusing on what went well and the impact it had. Then, you ask for their feedback on how to engage more volunteers for future events and any advice on managing resources more effectively. This opens up a constructive dialogue, providing you with valuable insights for improvement.

Recognizing a Colleague's Effort

Celebrate Others' Victories Too: A colleague shares with you their success in solving a long-standing issue with a client. You genuinely congratulate them and take a moment to highlight their achievement in the next team meeting, acknowledging their hard work and dedication. This gesture strengthens your relationship and encourages a culture of recognition within the team.

Sharing on Social Media

Use Social Media Wisely: After months of practicing, you finally achieve a personal best in running. You decide to share this victory on social media, not just as a brag but to inspire others on their fitness journey. You post a before-and-after picture, detailing your training regimen, the ups and downs, and how you stayed motivated. The post receives positive engagement, with others sharing their stories and seeking advice, turning your personal victory into inspiration for a community.

Conclusion

Applying these tips and strategies to share your unseen victories can enrich your relationships, foster a supportive community, and inspire others to recognize and celebrate their own achievements. Whether it's through personal conversations, at work, or on social media, sharing your victories with honesty, humility, and a sense of community can make a significant difference in how we perceive and celebrate success.

Here's a quick rundown:

1. Talk to people who support you about the small but significant steps you've taken towards your goals.

2. Stay humble when you share, focusing on the journey and the team effort rather than just your own win.

3. Tell the whole story, not just the end result, to really connect with others and maybe inspire them.

4. Ask for feedback after you share your win, to start a conversation and maybe learn something new.

5. Celebrate other people's wins as much as your own to build a positive vibe and stronger relationships.

6. Share wisely on social media to inspire others and create a community of positivity and support.

By following these tips, you can make sharing your unseen victories a way to connect deeper with others, inspire them, and build a circle where everyone feels valued and supported. It's all about making the little moments count and spreading the good vibes around.

Celebrating Your Unseen Victories

TIME TO LEARN THE importance of celebrating your small achievements, as well as the hidden power they hold in shaping your path to success. When you recognize the value of your unseen victories, you are able to boost your self-confidence and motivation, ultimately propelling you towards your goals.

Journey to Self-Discovery

Embracing your journey of self-discovery and growth is about appreciating the process of learning who you are and what you're capable of. It's not just about reaching a destination but about the experiences and insights gained along the way. This path encourages you to explore your passions, challenge your limits, and evolve continuously. By valuing each step of this journey, you cultivate a deeper understanding of yourself and a stronger foundation for personal success.

Small Steps, Big Value

Recognizing the value of small steps towards progress emphasizes the importance of every effort you make on your path to success. These incremental achievements might seem insignificant when viewed in isolation, but they cumulatively lead to substantial growth and improvement. Celebrating these small victories keeps you motivated and focused, reminding you that every action contributes to your larger goals.

Positivity and Resilience

Harnessing the power of positivity and resilience in achieving success is about maintaining an optimistic outlook and bouncing back from setbacks. Positivity fuels your drive and determination, while resilience ensures you can withstand and learn from the inevitable obstacles and challenges. Together, they empower you to pursue your goals with confidence, turning adversity into opportunity.

Overcoming Challenges

Finding strength in overcoming obstacles and challenges highlights the importance of resilience and perseverance on your path to success. Every challenge you face and conquer strengthens your character and equips you with valuable lessons and experiences. This process not only contributes to your personal and professional growth but also builds a robust foundation for future achievements.

Celebrating Growth

Celebrating personal growth and development along the way is about acknowledging and taking pride in your evolution. It's recognizing that your journey to success is as much about who you become as it is about what you achieve. By valuing your growth, you honor the hard work, dedication, and transformation that define your path, reinforcing the belief in your potential and the journey itself.

Conclusion

Embracing the journey of self-discovery and growth is a fundamental aspect of personal development. It is about exploring and understanding oneself, facing one's fears and insecurities, and constantly striving to become the best version of oneself This journey is not always easy, but it is incredibly rewarding. By stepping out of our comfort zones and embracing new experiences, we open ourselves up to endless possibilities for growth and self-improvement.

Recognizing the value of small steps towards progress is essential in achieving long-term success. Oftentimes, we may feel overwhelmed by the enormity of our goals and dreams. However, by breaking them down into smaller, more manageable tasks, we can take consistent and meaningful steps towards our desired outcomes. Every small achievement, no matter how seemingly insignificant, brings us one step closer to reaching our ultimate goals. By focusing on the things we are thankful for and acknowledging our own strengths and accomplishments, we can boost our self-esteem and overall well-being.

Harnessing the power of positivity and resilience is key in overcoming obstacles and achieving success. Life is full of challenges and setbacks, but by maintaining a positive attitude and bouncing back from failures, we can persevere and continue moving forward. Resilience is the ability to adapt and thrive in the face of adversity, and it is a skill that can be developed through practice and self-reflection. Finding strength in overcoming obstacles and challenges is a testament to our resilience and determination. Each hurdle we overcome builds our confidence and inner strength, preparing us for future challenges that may come our way.

By viewing obstacles as opportunities for growth and learning, we can transform setbacks into stepping stones towards success. Celebrating personal growth and development along the way is essential in staying motivated and inspired on our journey towards self-improvement. It is important to acknowledge and celebrate our achievements, no matter how small, as they are a reflection of our hard work and dedication. By recognizing and honoring our progress, we can stay motivated and inspired to continue pushing ourselves towards our goals and dreams.

About the author

Juliet Agocha is a renowned figure in the leadership realm, her contributions leaving an indelible mark on the field. Internationally acclaimed for her immersive and transformative approach to leadership, Juliet's expertise shines through her inspirational book, "7 Ways to Overcome Fear." Beyond her literary prowess, she also serves as the CEO of the technology company, Ultimate Web Design.

Juliet's educational journey is a testament to her unwavering pursuit of knowledge. She holds a bachelor's degree in information technology from Columbia Southern University, Alabama, a master's in Cybersecurity with honors from American Public University, West Virginia. and a Ph.D. candidate at the University of Cumberland, Kentuky, USA.

A lifelong learner and prolific mentor, Juliet guides individuals through the intricacies of personal growth, helping them navigate difficult challenges, make informed decisions, and unlock their full potential. Her inspirational speaking engagements empower both men and women to embrace self-improvement and overcome obstacles with resilience and determination.

www.ingramcontent.com/pod-product-compliance
Lightning Source LLC
Chambersburg PA
CBHW071512150726
48000CB00002B/548